# A Poetic Conversation

## The ACTs of life

To Lee,

Welcome to the Conversation

*Darryl Gaines*

## Poetry from the heart

# BY DARRYL GAINES
## Devine Poet

ISBN-10:1-945532-47-5
ISBN-13:978-1-945532-47-4

Published by Opportune Independent Publishing Co.
Cover, Editing & Formatting by Opportune Independent Publishing Co.

*Printed in the United States of America*

For permission requests, write to the Opportune Publishing addressed "Attention: Permissions Coordinator" to the address below.

*113 Live Oak Street*
*Houston, TX 77003*
*(832) 263-1700*
*Info@opportunepublishing.com*
*www.opportunepublishing.com*

*Portions of the proceeds from the sale of this book will be donated to the Darryl Gaines Foundation.*

**VISION**
The Darryl Gaines Foundation will endeavor to shape 21st Century leaders, uplift vulnerable communities, and provide a pathway towards success.

**MISSION**
The Darryl Gaines Foundation seeks to address the challenges facing vulnerable communities, to improve existing youth programs and initiatives, and to provide awareness of careers in Science, Technology, Engineering, and Mathematics (STEM).

**PURPOSE**
To develop key partnerships with local business, government and community leaders;
To conduct camps to promote life skills, health awareness and STEM education;
To strengthen existing community programs and initiatives; and
To provide scholarships and tuition assistance.

# ACKNOWLEDGEMENT

I want to honor God—who provides, loves and forgives all unconditionally. I am assuredly a prodigal son, made many mistakes, imperfect in many ways, this I know is my truth. But God continues to polish, shine and sharpen me day by day, and for that, I admire, love and thank him for who He is in my life. I want to thank my mother for her unconditional love and friendship. To everyone who at some point became part of my journey and an inspiration for these words of poetry, may God continue to bless your life and journey.

I would like to thank my mentors and coaches, both personal and professional, who have challenged me to be and do my best over the years. And, most importantly, to reach back and bring others along the way. The saying goes, you can tell the character of a man by the friends he keeps. Albert G. Edwards and Dr. Samuel L. Johnson, are at the top of that list and most certainly make me aware and accountable for my actions.

Thanks to my children, Olivia, Darryl Jr., Nile and Devin whom I so dearly treasure and love with all of my heart.

To all who were so gracious in pre-reading and giving me honest feedback, I thank you. Thanks to Niedra Kenny and Natalie Poole for assisting me from the beginning and giving me that extra push I needed.

My life isn't so different from those who have come from a meager background and who have put in the work because of the desire to succeed and show those who follow the extent to which they can also be successful if they tried.

**_DARE to DREAM and DREAM BIG_**

# FOREWORD

It is said that most poems are written from the authors own personal experience. If this is true, then Darryl Gaines has an extensive wrath of knowledge to draw from. I've known him personally for over 30 years, and in all those years I've found him to be a masterful storyteller—poetic justice.

To master the English language is a gift. Darryl has taken his love of the language and his experiences of a lifetime and meshed them together, taking us on an enjoyable poetic ride. His personal journey has been long and arduous. His determination to survive at all cost is elegantly laid out here. His brilliance of having beautifully molded them into poetic prose makes for a great read and an appreciation of the struggles he's had to endure to reach the pinnacle he finds himself at today. The degree of love, as well as the scope and depth of these poems, will leave you in awe; as well as inspired.

I commend him on a job well done. It is my sincere hope that you'll find this collection of his life's events as inspirational as I have, it is well worth the read.

—John Martin Branson III

# A MESSAGE TO THE WORLD

## **<u>LOVE IS</u>**

Love is knowing just who you are
With God in your spirit and soul
Relinquishing all control of yourself,
As your needs are put on hold,

Love is what you do,
In spite of things gone wrong,
Holding your trust in God,
His will becomes your own,

Love is speaking words on high
When you're feeling lost and low
Facing unforgiving storms
While standing tall and bold

Love is letting others chose
When it's not what you believe
It's not about what you want
Or even what you perceive

Love is holding on to hearts
Desperately needing to be held
And letting go when the time is right
So you can watch them as they sail

Love is hearing sounds of pain
A voice abounds with grief
Listening without saying a word
As they speak themselves into peace

And yet Love is simply timeless
A precious gift of life
Set in our hearts and minds at birth
As we chose between wrong and right

# INTRODUCTION
# THE ACTS

By capturing Love, Spirit and Inspiration in each moment during my life, I hope they will make a difference in at least one other person's life—for that is the measure of Gods success through me, the journey of choice and ACTs that I have endeavored and placed in this book of poetry.

I have given a voice to the words that describe my life as ACTs in this book.

**In Love:**
**1 John 4:7 - Beloved, let us love one another: for love is of God; and everyone that loveth is born of God, and knoweth God.**

**In Spirit:**
**Matthew 6:33 - But seek ye first the kingdom of God, and his righteousness; and all these things shall be added unto you.**

**Inspired:**
**Philippians 4:13 - I can do all things through Christ who strengthens me.**

# TABLE OF CONTENTS

## *Act 3*

# ACT 1

## In Love

**1 John 4:7**

Beloved, let us love one another: for love is of God; and everyone that loveth is born of God, and knoweth God.

*Love*

Angels are those who surround you and make life just
a little better. Those who believe in you, love you and genuinely
care about your well-being.

# AN ANGEL

An Angel, that's what you are to me
A sweetness arising out of my dream, out of my sleep

An Angel, that's what you are to me
A blessing from above, for all my eternity

An Angel, that's what you are to me
Just as I was fading, you arrived and set my soul free

An Angel, that's what you are to me
The essence of love, to ease my pain wherever it may be

An Angel, that's what you are to me
Dwelling deep within, knowing what I feel and seeing what I see

An Angel, that's what you are to me
The strength of my journey, the light of my destiny

An Angel, that's what you are to me
My very own Angel, giving me life, hope and love indeed

An Angel, that's what you are to me
A sweet and gentle touch, to hold me when I'm in need

An Angel, that's what you are to me
Lifting my spirit, giving me harmony, giving me peace

An Angel, that's what you are to me

# *Love*

When you meet someone, and you both
feel a connection—carefree and open. It's like a dance,
a rhythm, a moment when you are both in sync.

# Dancing in the Rain

As I stand back, arms folded watching as best I can
The rain pours, the sun shines, as we're caught without a chance

Your silhouette drenched from head to toe,
your smile so beautiful and true
My heart begins to pound. My hands begin to reach. My feet begin to move

Our eyes touch for only a moment, as our hearts beat on pace
Such beautiful motion going round and round,
while drops fall softly on your face

You have made me smile if just for a while, your spirit moves me inside
Your caress is sweet as we move our feet, treading side by side slowly

I can see it in your face your smile so filled with grace,
and passion for what you do
You've shared with me, you've set me free, and for that, I give thanks to you

Your song comes to an end, while you dance right through the wind,
as I stand back and watch you dance once again

In the Rain

# Love

Spiritual connectivity, a journey for two
with God's will leading the way.

# GOD MADE US

God made us to see each other through His eyes
God made us to know each other through His mind

God made us to feel each other through His heart
God made us to be one and set us apart

God made us to believe in Him through His faith
God made us from love and freed us from hate

God made us a part of Him through His soul
God made us for heavenly treasures untold

God made us to know His will through His Son
God made us to forsake all and always be one

God made us
And we are His blessing

*Love*

When you meet someone who exemplifies
all those things dearest to your heart & mind, it's like heaven.

# Heaven

You are heaven, yes, you are heaven to me
Flowing in my mind so freely, so wonderfully
Exactly what I want, what I need, you are heaven indeed
Far above what my mind can see, deep within the heart of me
You are heaven, yes, you are heaven to me
A treasure of love waiting for release, to be set free
Captive only for a moment, to indulge in loves insanity
But always aware that truth will always and surely set one free
You are heaven, yes, you are heaven to me
Like a beautiful flower, birthing and rising to share its story
Like its peddles you are sweet, your emotions are as tear drops laying softly
And yet your patience, your love abides Gods truth and wisest glory
You are heaven, yes, you are heaven to me
Like the voice of a bird, you sing so sweetly
Sounds filled with passion makes my heart tingle constantly
You bring joy into my life. You give me the strength I need to be me
You are heaven, yes, you are heaven to me
Absolutely beautiful you are, so tender, sharing you, affectionately
Just being close to you heaven, I rise, yes I rise, my desire uncontrollably
Words or poems cannot truly express the deepness of you inside of me
You are truly heaven, yes, you are heaven to me
The best thing I've ever had in this life, so sweet so naturally
You give me comfort away from my troubles, with you I sleep so easily
When I think about you heaven, I am free from what life brings to me
So you are heaven, yes, you are nothing but sweet heaven to me
That's what you will always be, for a lifetime of you is my eternity
My dreams have become so alive, so vivid, flowing over my heart as it beats
What else is there besides loving you, passionately, deeply, affectionately

You are heaven, yes, you are heaven to me

*Love*

A moment of happiness with the one you love
in peace and quiet, even in slumber, enjoy each moment.

# As I Watch You Sleep

As I gaze at your beauty, so soft, so deep
I realize my treasure, as I watch you sleep
Your heart so true, as I listen for a sound
A smile on my face, as you reach around
On my chest, then my side, you finally found
A place just right and asleep you went, sound
I feel your peace, so still, so calm
As I watch you sleep so beautiful in my arms
Happy is my heart, full of love and true as yours
As I watch you sleep, for it's you I adore

For God said, "Therefore a man shall leave his father and his
mother and hold fast to his wife, and they shall become one flesh."

# I Do

A special day will soon be here. Our hearts grow near, our love so dear.
the joy, the smiles, the peace we keep, our love has grown ever so deep

I love you. I always will. This is my gift from me to you, my heart is
filled with joy, as we say "I DO"

Days will come, time will pass, this love we share through time will last
sweet words we say, each time we part
I love you, be safe, straight from the Heart

I love you. I always will. This is my gift from me to you, my heart is
filled with joy, as we say "I DO"

On our knees we will pray, each and every night
through our ups and downs, he will keep us in his sight

As we stand here together to share this precious day
giving our lives to each other in a very special way

I love you. I always will. This is my gift from me to you, my heart is
filled with joy, as we say "I DO"

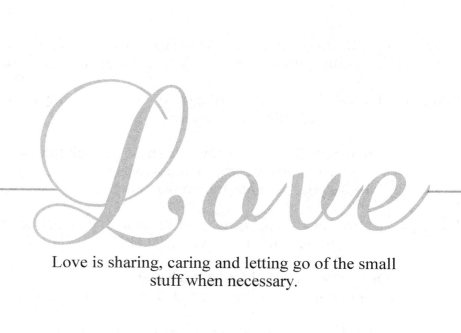

*Love*

Love is sharing, caring and letting go of the small
stuff when necessary.

# LOVE

Love is two people sharing life forever
Love is sticking it out and staying together

Love is two hearts with the same feeling
Love is listening when it's time for healing

Love is always doing things for each other
Love is compromising self for the other

Love is dreaming the very same vision
Love is talking to make a decision

But above all
Love is two hearts beating as one
And never missing a beat

# Love

Making love is more than a physical act when
you truly love someone.

# <u>Making Love To You Is A Frame Of Mind</u>

Making love to you is a frame of mind, best served anywhere with lots of time. It's all around us, happens every day, in multiple places, in multiple ways.

Making love to you is a frame of mind, it's pure and sweet, it's truly divine, no matter the weather, rain or shine, to be close to each other, a reason we'll find.

Making love to you is a frame of mind, my soul and yours are truly entwined, our spirits do touch each other every time.

Making love to you is a frame of mind, sometimes we forget even lose track of time, two hearts beating on pace, a sound so divine, while making love in one frame of mind

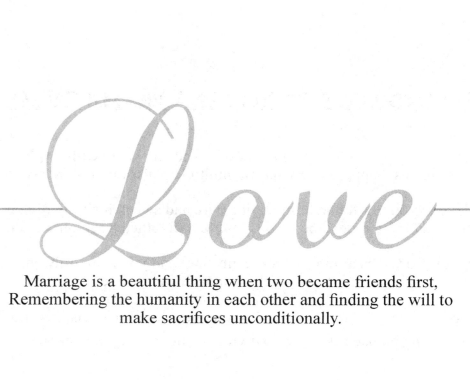

Marriage is a beautiful thing when two became friends first,
Remembering the humanity in each other and finding the will to
make sacrifices unconditionally.

# Marry You Again

I would marry you again, again and again
Without hesitation, without family or even friends
Marrying you again, so sweet it sounds to me
Only God knows, the joy and love there will be

I would marry you again, again and again
Knowing what I know now
Knowing what I knew then
You are my friend, my love and my life
For these are the reasons, you became my wife

I would marry you again, again and again
For your spirit is true, as I look within
Through patience and time, Gods work has been done
He has blessed our love, as we both became one

*Love*

The joy of being in love at its best will draw upon your
spirit and heart felt dreams to bring peace to your life.

# <u>My Dream of You</u>

My dream of you is filled with love
It's made of things from God above
With joy and peace and every delight
It ebbs and flows but always ends right

I close my eyes as you close yours
We journey together, along beaches and shores
Our souls share love while we're apart
This is my dream, and it comes from my heart

Oh, what a dream to have come true
It is what God meant when He gave me to you
Again, and again this dream I would do
To spend the rest of my life with you

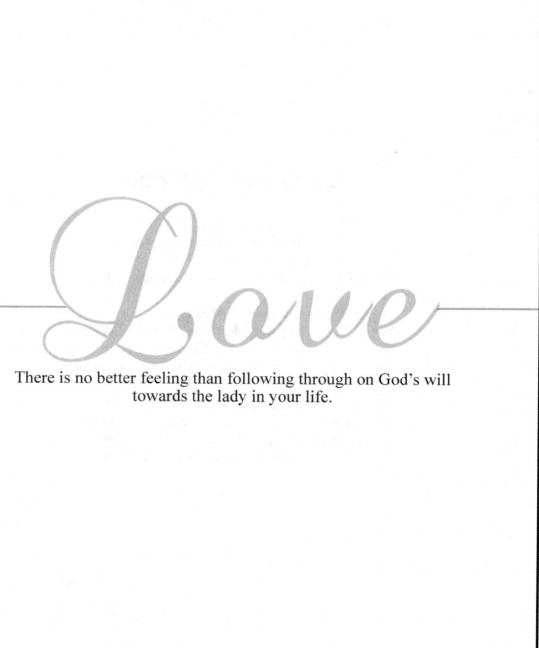

*Love*

There is no better feeling than following through on God's will towards the lady in your life.

# My Queen

When I awake each morning new, open my eyes and look at you, I'm blessed again to see your face; I stare for a moment as you awake, A kiss from you in the morning glare, true love and peace we seem to share,

You are my queen, my beautiful dream, uplifting my soul, my everything

You give your heart to those in pain, embracing their hurt just the same, so much strength, such a wonderful lady, never losing control when things get crazy, full of wisdom, love and grace, my pride and joy, you can never be replaced,

You are my queen, my beautiful dream, uplifting my soul, my everything

Not a day goes by, neither dusk nor dawn, without your love, your touch so warm You make my life worth living each and every day, you make it worth my time Can't imagine being without your love, all alone, I would lose my mind

You are my queen, my beautiful dream, uplifting my soul, my everything

*Love*

Sharing love and joining souls begins the journey of a
lifetime for those willing to hold on to each other.

# OUR JOURNEY BEGINS

And now we are here as true as can be
For I love you and you love me
Our life now begins, a journey for all to see
As we travel the way, just you and me

What a love we share from dusk to dawn
Your spirit so sweet, makes me rush to get home
For the time we spend in each other's arms
Makes things right no matter how bad
No matter the harm

It was chosen, our path, before we both began
He brought me to you and gave me your hand
With you and I whole, from now until then
Two hearts, two souls, now one to the end

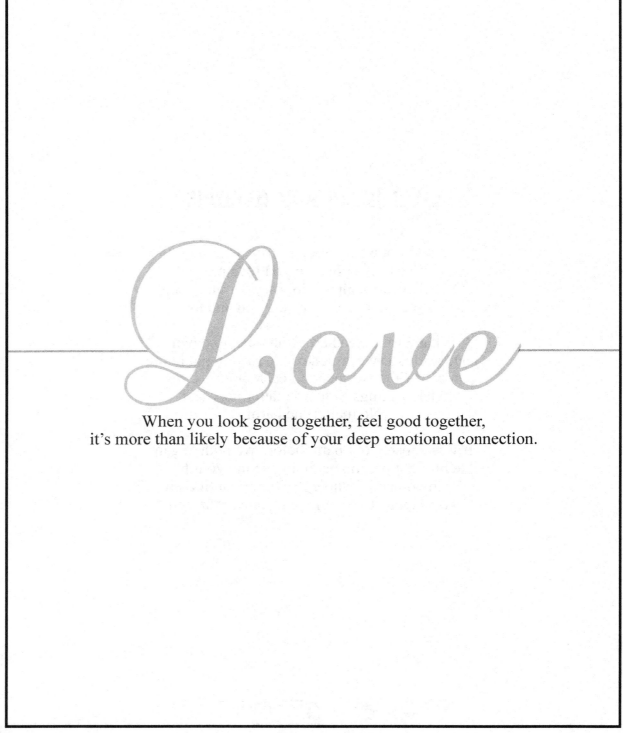

*Love*

When you look good together, feel good together,
it's more than likely because of your deep emotional connection.

# Soul Mates

Souls that mate happen once in a chance
I try to breathe, but I am covered in romance
Lost control of my soul in faith,
I believe he will make this sweet to our taste
It is true. It is real, it is honest and forever
We are blessed to have each other, for now, and forever
Many times it may seem uphill as we go
We will endure with love and faith for the world to know

May god keep us together forever

What would you do to become one in mind, sprint &
body, the journey together would be love.

# What I Would Do

I would stir your emotions set your soul on fire,
Take you to a new life awaken in you a new desire
I would love you beyond imaginations in your mind
Fill your heart, breathe your air as if it were mine

I would give you all of me to have and to hold
Anything I would do for you from deep within my soul
I would reach for you if you begin to fade
Give you my love, my essence, for you are the reason I was made

I would touch your soul in moment's breath of time
Give you all of my spiritual wealth just to make you mine
I would bring you into my world for ever in this life
Never will I leave you or desert you out of spite

I would make your dreams my dreams for all to see
Keep you close to my heart, where you will always be
That's what I would do

*Love*

The greatest friendship begins with openness and the
willingness to be vulnerable.

# A Piece of Me

Always I am in your path on your way to destiny
In your way, I stand arms wide open to give you a piece of me

A day's worth of my dreams, thoughts and hopes you always seem to be
In this moment, my heart and soul I give to you a piece of me

My baby, my love, my lady, your spirit and mine always in love indeed
Miles can only separate physically, but I keep for you a piece of me

Making love to the sound of your voice a whisper so clear to me
Deep in my heart I feel your love, I feel you touching just a piece of me

No other love have I shared my deepest thoughts, my cares, all of my needs
Always you're willing to share in my pain
So forever I keep for you a piece of me

And so you have always played a part in my life,
Given me your best you set me free
Just place me firmly in your heart next to your soul, and I will always share a piece of
me

*Love*

Always remember to take care of each other.

# CANDLE LIGHT

There is a light inside that shines so bright
Its flame is true, its flame is right
May we keep these flames as they burn through time
There's a flame for you and one that's mine
As we journey through this life, we must always share the flame
To help others who only flicker as they deal with their own pain
You should always trim your wick, and I will do the same
Let our lights shine before God, in Jesus holy name

*Love*

Remember God—Pray for his guidance.

# IF WE MET GOD TODAY

If we met God today would we fall down on our knees to pray
Or would it be too late for anything we had to say

Would we thank him for his patience, mercy and unshaken grace
Or would we try our best to hide in some secret place

If we met God today would he smile with joy for our faith
Or would he lower his head from our total disgrace

Would we ask him for forgiveness for the days we displayed hate
Or would we say I'm sorry cause we didn't finish the race

If we met God today would we have lived selfishly as mates
Or unconditionally loved one another through pain and heartache

If we have been good and faithful servants in God's Holy way
He'd say, "Here in my heaven, I have built you a brand-new place."

Love will be what the two of you perceive it to be.

# Imagine That

In the midst of a dream, true spirits do attract
Two souls, two lives, deep in love
Imagine That

Our hearts give love and love comes back
We believe in each other
Imagine That

Love laid me in your heart I can never turn back
Miles I travel just to see you smile
Imagine That

One day we say those words, that bind our souls intact
Our journey begins with love
Imagine That

# SPEAK YOUR TRUTH ABOUT
# LOVE

Which of the poems in this ACT inspired you the most?
How has this ACT encouraged you to speak the truth about love in your life?

*You may ask me a question about this ACT or leave a thought at: darrylgaines.com/Books*

# ACT 2

**Matthew 6:33**

But seek ye first the kingdom of God, and his righteousness; and all these things shall be added unto you.

*Spirit*

Gods spirit is in everyone. Listen for it,
and it will guide you.

# THE SPIRIT IN ME

Covered in flesh so no one can see
The things I go through while God whispers to me

As time passes my conscience awakens
And joins the journey to set me free

Awareness of these allows me to see
My path towards victory

That every moment is an opportunity to do God's will
And to separate myself spiritually

From the highs and lows, the hurt and pain, knowing full well
That this is what he desires for my spiritual gain

To look beyond myself,
to reach out and bring forth other souls that have failed
To give love and forgiveness off the chart, off the scale

The spirit inside me, with my conscience and awareness in hand
Knowing I can do all things through God as a man

By simply believing in him in exchange for setting my soul free
Forgiving me, again and again, each time I fall short of his will inside of me

Spiritually, inside of me.

I am free

# *Spirit*

Moments in time, are all we have. Stop for
a moment and breathe.

# BREATH OF FRESH AIR

A Breath of fresh air, my heart's sweetest desire
To rest and cool my feet from this journey by fire
I made no qualms as I moved diligently through time
I gave all I could, when I could, even if I fell behind

Oh, this breath of fresh air is so soothing to my soul
As I ascend with angels feet and hands shining bright as gold
I see what glory came from tired and shaking hands
Until my last waking moment

Nothing I've done, Nothing I've said, I care to hold or hide
I walked in love and victory now I sit by the Master's side
My faith I held unfailingly, my love I gave true and strong
The unselfish prayers I prayed are what brought my spirit home

# Spirit

Prayer is the beginning of humility and the
end of total self-reliance.

# I PRAYED LAST NIGHT

I prayed last night, didn't ask for a thing
Just wanted him to know, he's still my king

I prayed last night, didn't say one word
Just wanted him to know, his will I serve

I prayed last night, gave thanks for his blessing
Just wanted him to know, I've learned my lesson

I prayed last night, opened up my heart
Just wanted him to know, my faith will never part

I prayed last night, just wanted him to know
My spirit, my soul, he has all control

*Spirit*

Are you ready if you get called today?

# If You Met God Today

If you met God today would you fall down on your knees to pray
Or would it be too late for anything you have to say

Would you thank him for his patience, mercy and unshaken grace
Or would you try your best to hide in some secret place

If you met God today would he smile with joy from your embrace
Or would he lower his head from your total disgrace

Would you ask him for forgiveness for the days you had no faith
Or would you say I'm sorry cause you didn't finish the race

If you met God today would he know you've given grace and prayed for those in need
and given them the wisdom to live his holy way

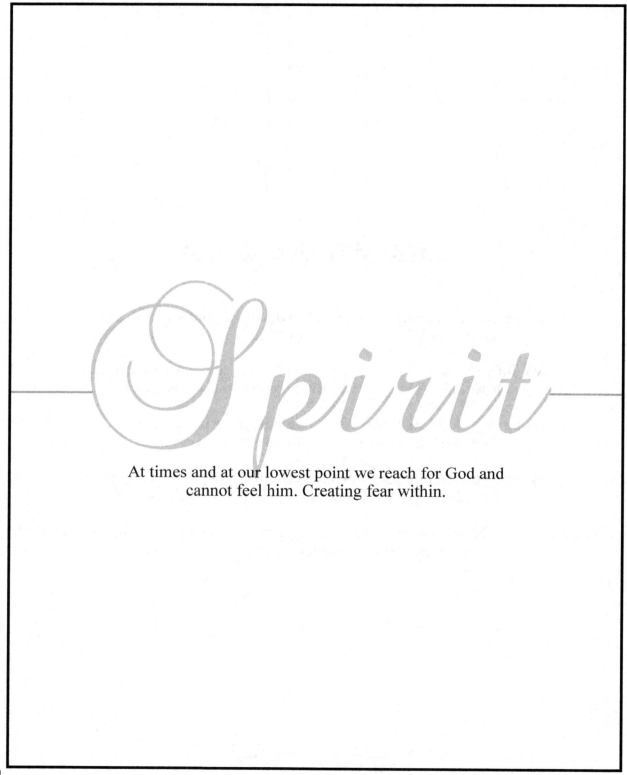

Spirit

At times and at our lowest point we reach for God and
cannot feel him. Creating fear within.

# Lord Is There A Reason Why

Lord is there a reason why I came to be, is there a reason why
I can't seem to see, what you meant for me, I can't see why
Every day goes by, so swiftly to me, no matter how hard I try
I see everything again and again, as each day goes passing by
So, I ask you again, from deep within, can you please try
Lord, I ask you please, just share with me, the reason why
Lord my love runs deep, from soul to soul and I'm not afraid or even shy
I'll tell anyone, about what you've done, to save my selfish, sinful life
From time to time I hear your voice, it must be you. I just don't know why
And even though I trust what you say, my flesh is weak,
no matter how hard I try, it gets the best of me
So, I ask you again, from deep within, can you please try
Lord, I ask you please, just share with me, the reason why
Time and time again, I give my heart to those in need
could this be the reason why I came to be
So easy for me, to set them free, of hurt and pain
you gave that to me I can't deny
maybe that's the reason why

*Spirit*

Sow seeds together and reap double portions
of God's goodness.

## It Ain't About We

GOD made us both unselfishly
To give and to love purposely

What we want, what we need
Does it matter, it ain't about we

The things we need come from our seed
So, he gave me to you, and you to me

So, we could understand

it ain't about we.

*Spirit*

Step back when life throws you a curve ball assess
the situation and move with caution.

# Let Your Soul Be Still

Give hold to the words of God, be blessed, be bold
For his answer to the spirited heart will never go untold
Trust in his way, be strong and live in his will
Listen to your spirit let your soul be still
There's a light he left just for you
Reach within his words, they're blessed, they're true
In the midst of a storm filled with troubles beset with ill's
Listen to your spirit let your soul be still
The day of your awakening will be one of love and unshakeable faith
Your belief grows beyond measure, your spirit beyond self and hate
Nothing in the natural will control your thoughts, your actions or your will

Because you've mastered listening to your spirit and letting your soul be still

*Spirit*

Know that every moment of your life is as important
as the next, so live now at your best.

# Live Today

Live today as if there was nothing you couldn't possess
A complete journey from birth to death
Live today as if it were the last piece of a puzzle
A drink of Gods water, to end all of your troubles
Live today as if God touched your heart and opened your eyes with purpose
A day of love and patience that quenched all your thirst
Know that today is only a moment with God in mind
Live today as if it is the very first grain of sand in the hour glass of time

*Spirit*

Be thankful for existence but most of all for
everything you experience both good and bad.

# THANK YOU, LORD

Thank you, Lord, for waking me to see your glorious sun rise
For lifting me up and opening my spiritual eyes

Thank you, Lord, for such a wonderful gift of life
To share what you've placed in my heart and soul so deep inside

Thank you, Lord, for love, peace and happiness
For guiding my life as you know best

Thank you, Lord, for pain, suffering and even strife
For they make me strong and wise to do battle in my spiritual fight

Thank you, Lord, for in spite of all I do, think and say wrong
Your arms are always open for me to come home

I thank you, Lord, for who you are in me

*Spirit*

When you realize that God walks with you,
your confidence grows tremendously.

# WALKiN ON WATER

I am light, drifting on your every word
feeling your air underneath my arms spread wide
Every step I take assured and firm as the next
lifting me above the waves no fear inside
Got me WalkiN on Water gracefully in step, peacefully in stride
Swept away by the rush of vibrations coming into view
setting my heart on fire my soul anew
Clearing my mind of any and all negative thoughts and desires
giving me new things to do
Got me WalkiN on Water, gracefully showing love
peacefully accepting my truth
Moving in a new space, shedding the past, opening my heart and soul wide
Bringing new life to those who desire, healing those with hurt
mending the broken inside
Got me WalkiN on Water gracefully in step, peacefully in stride
Speaking the unspoken words, living my hearts desires
my intentions ringing out, authentically true
Unafraid to walk on this water, this path,
My heart and mind  as one, with faith there is nothing I can't do

*Spirit*

God's will is much greater and in turn,
provides more fulfillment.

# YOUR WILL HIS WILL

In your eyes, I see your very own dreams
To be loved is your wish, this is what I have seen
You try so hard; you try to please
You give your heart and your body with ease

If only you knew, the truth in this thing
The path that you seek, this wish, this dream
Will only come true, when you fully become whole
Take care of yourself; God gave you a soul

When you begin to see his will
He'll open your eyes, your heart he will fill
With joy and peace, with love and happiness
Give your love to him, and he'll do the rest
But you must first find the safest place within
To keep his will, trust in him and only then will your life  begin

# SPEAK YOUR TRUTH ABOUT
# SPIRIT

Which of the poems in this ACT inspired you the most?
How has this ACT encouraged you to speak the truth about spirit in your life?

*You may ask me a question about this ACT or leave a thought at: darrylgaines.com/Books*

# ACT 3

## Inspired

**Philippians 4:13**

I can do all things through Christ who strengthens me.

# Inspired

My Greatest Inspiration

# MY MOTHER

Words cannot describe the love I have for you in my heart, nestled deep inside
Nothing I can do will ever be enough to repay you
never catch up, too far behind
You gave me life, you showed me compassion and truth, so I never lose sight
honoring you, I am blessed in my very own way, as I rise to higher heights


Because
you are a beautiful flower, a butterfly, a calming voice to rest my soul
In a world full of storms, full of valleys, you always find me when I'm lost and cold,
Cause you, yes you are my mother


I never understand how you do so much, give so much, every bit of your last
Never saying a harsh word when it never returns but always ready to give half
You gave me a gift, one that I can assuredly never in this lifetime repay
You gave me eyes to see, ears to hear
hands to touch and lips for the words I must say


Because
you are a beautiful flower, a butterfly, a calming voice to rest my soul
In a world full of storms, full of valleys, you always find me when I'm lost and cold,
Cause you, yes you are my mother


I know this to be truth, God is on everything I do, every movement I make
I keep it that way because you told me if I walk with him he will show me the way
Nothing is closer to me than your heart, your smile
the warmth of your hug when I am away
Just the thought of you sometimes can ease my nerves
calm my spirit take the hurt away


Because
you are a beautiful flower, a butterfly, a calming voice to rest my soul
In a world full of storms, full of valleys, you always find me when I'm lost and cold,
Cause you, yes you are my mother

# Inspired

A heartfelt lasting impression of a woman working hard and staying the course because triumph is near.

# Little Lady Making Due

Hey you, little lady making due
Let me tell you something, get ready for what Gods about to do
From my view, what I see in you
You're something special, little lady making due
Hey you, little lady making due
Selfless, deep love underneath, tireless that's you
Trusting no one fully from what life's put you through
You're something wonderful, little lady making due
Hey you, little lady making due
You gave birth, shared the fruits inside of you
Lives touched by you, lives you will always be connected to
You're something beautiful, little lady making due
Hey you, little lady making due
Champagne, caviar, your desires are coming true
What a blessing you are, a life to share, love just being next to you
You're something true, little lady making due
Hey you, little lady making due
Someone's on your side, going to help you see it through
Got your back, filling the gap with love and truth
You're something special, little lady making due

# Inspired

You have everything you need inside, but lean on
others when you need to.

# STRENGTH WITHIN

Strength my dear comes from within
Sit still, listen and you'll begin
To know the strength, you have inside
The soul you keep, you cannot hide
Just know that I am here for you
Right here is where I'll be, always
When times are tough, and you need someone
Just come and lean on me.
Strength my dear comes from within
It's buried deep inside,
It's past the problems on your heart
It's past your fear and pride
So, journey to that place inside
I'll show you what to do
And if you stumble I'll share my strength
Just trust me I'm here for you.

# Inspired

Walk by faith, not by sight. Simple but true.

# FAITHFUL JOURNEY

In the blackness of time are moments of choice
A faithful journey will prove to be a wise and trustworthy voice
Passionate desires without bounds, control or even thought
A faithful journey cools the soul inside and out
Life will continually try and measure one's trust and belief
A faithful journey gives peace well beyond heartache and grief
A chasm of knowledge may change or alter your way
Yet a faithful journey in truth and love never goes astray
Every step you take is a brush stroke of your life's visible portrait
A faithful journey unfinished on canvas, but beautifully draped
Understanding and wisdom birthed through experience and time
A faithful journey will raise one's spirit, will raise one's mind
Desperately we seek our true purpose in this space and time
A faithful journey in God reveals his insight as well as his signs
So be aware and listen closely weighing both heart and mind
And faithfully journey eyes wide open listening for those whispering guides

# Inspired

Slow down and enjoy life, release the stress.

# Go Through Life

If you go through life, at the speed of sound
It won't make sense when it all slows down


If you go through life, in bits and pieces
It won't make sense, without logic or reason


If you go through life, always in doubt
You'll never understand what it's all about


If you go through life, and can't remember a face
Do you really know, why you're in this place


If you go through life, and you know who you are
Share with someone, the choices you made to get so far
Going through life

# Inspired

We can all bring hope to the world.

# I Am Hope

I am hope, when I see through the mountain and view a higher prize
I am hope, when I armor up, stand up and rise
I am Hope, when I walk the path no matter how high
I am Hope, when I push through the obstacles in my mind
I am Hope, when I never give up knowing what's on the other side
I am Hope, when I stand on top shine my light so others can decide
I am Hope, when I reach out and pull others who have fallen aside
I am Hope, I am love because GOD has opened my eyes
I am hope, I will share his gifts, for he has made me wise
I am Hope, because I dare to dream beyond my imagination and time
I am Hope, as I walk the path least desired, unafraid, leaving trails opened wide
I am Hope, I am humility, authentically in service to God
learning and share his message, we are all one and full of his Love

# Inspired

Be a warrior for God—Armor up.

# I Am the One

I am the one who gives love unconditionally
I set lost and lonely souls free, yes that's me
I am uncontrollably the master's work undoubtedly
I work only for him in this plane of eternity
I express his vision of love and forgiveness so aggressively
I am the one, yes that's me
If for some reason you don't believe, bring it on and try me
I got the word as my sword, the heart of a lion, full of tenacity
I walk this world literally with the spirit guiding me
Listening to God's heartbeat inside of me
I am the one, yes that's me
Watching with spiritual eyes the natural world take place in front of me
I know without a doubt; the Lord is right here beside me
Where he's always been, where he'll always be
Helping me understand his will, he justified me, blessed me for eternity

I am the one, yes that's me

# Inspired

Selflessness brings humility and strength.

# I Give Myself

I give myself, and I give it free
To those in need who cannot see
I give them hope, a brand new dream
I give them strength, to do all things
I give myself to the meek and wise
If they only understand, I am their prize
If they believe in me and seek my way
They will sit next to me on that glorious day
I give myself from beginning to end
To help you through your pain and sin
I will build you up, I will make you strong
I will fill your needs if you sing my song
I give myself and you should too
Just remember my son
And what he would do
I will test your strengths, your will and your faith
Just remember my son and what he gave

# Inspired

Manhood requires a journey through good and bad.

# I Once Was A Boy

As I began my life new, A blank book what shall I do
Unaware of God's gift of choice, I chose what I felt what I knew
Life was good, and I owned the canvas and the colors too

I once was a boy, became a man, tried and true
Remembering the trail, I left behind to take me on to take me through
Never letting the height of the mountain sway me from what I needed to do
I press, and I press because I once was a boy, became a man tried and true

I loved and lost and never skipped a beat in time
never let life leave me behind
I trust only the spirit I possess for only it will be with me and for me
I continue to live and learn, never a thought of the end
for this life I love I yearn

I once was a boy, became a man, tried and true
Never forgetting the builders who laid bridges straight for me
The hands I held in my moments of grief
to steady my way in darkness when I could not see it through
I press, and I press because I once was a boy, became a man tried and true

I travel alone on this journey of mind
every step I take I chose until the end of time
Every word I share comes from my heart I give it freely in hopes that it returns in kind,
I listen for the truth, I seek the truth despite my fears I do with a smile

I once was a boy, became a man, tried and true
Through trials, tribulation and blues I became me in all I sought to do
I gave my flesh. I gave my blood, my peace and love as I grew
I press, and I press because I once was a boy, became a man tried and true

# Inspired

Don't get stuck with the same things, ways and
desires if you're not happy.

# IT'S TIME

You've done that before, don't go there no more
Find a way to move on, find a way to let go
It's time for a change, it's time you know
The path you've chosen doesn't seem to work
The words you've chosen, others they seem to hurt
It's time for a change, it's time to search
Get on your feet, you've had enough sleep
Don't stay where you are, you won't get too far
It's time for a change, time for a new start
Remember back then, way back when
Your heart was on fire, with so much desire
It's time for a change, time to be inspired
It's time, it's time, come on its time
Break free from what's now, put it all behind
It's time, it's time, come on its time
All the newness awaits you, will be yours in time
It's time for a change, you know it's time

# Inspired

Learn to control you, your destiny, your actions.

# Master of Mind

What I dream, what I think, what I believe I can do
Becomes my reality, divine desires come true
I rule my thoughts, I am my thoughts in time
I control my destiny, I am the master of mind
When I've lost my way, When I just don't know
I listen to my spirit, breathe, and search my soul
Faithful to my patience, knowing my path will shine
I watch, I lay, I sit still, I am the master of mind
I struggle to protect my purpose
To keep hold of my vision
Free will and choice, un-reflected
Attacking my decisions
I walk with peace, unafraid of what trouble I find
I understand my strength, I am the master of mind
I am blessed with gifts of faith, trust and true belief
For I have no worries or fears, as I rest or even sleep
I journey in search of vibrations
Both spiritual and divine
For they make me who I am
I am truly the master of mind

# Inspired

Your perception is your reality. Create your own success.

# My Existence

I walk this earth separated from the universal presence, in a vessel made to avail visions of life and time, a sense of pleasure, pain, hope and dreams.

I'm in a reality I continually create within my limited perception. My reality is what I believe, I struggle to hold on to this truth, trying to make sense of the things that happen to me daily, trying to be the good soldier, unable to predict the next incident to turn my world upside down without notice.

I have a sense of connectedness outside this world, I can't explain the feeling any more than that, but it's there, I feel it deep within. A knowing that there is a universal presence, beyond the limits of space and time, beyond anything we can imagine.

I often think if I let go of all of myself needs, my wants, my expectations, that I can somehow get synced with it and gain understanding beyond my present limitations gain an understanding of how to overcome the trials of life on earth and begin to unravel the true purpose of all things, as it exists, then navigate the universe and beyond.

Inspired

Be still and wait on God.

# PEACE BE STILL

In the midst of the storm
With your troubles and your ills
Listen to your spirit
He will set your soul still

He is there in your heart
He lives through your faith
He was there from the start
He'll help you through the space

He has a place just meant for you
Listen to his words
They're blessed
They're true

If you trust in him and his will
You'll listen when he tells you
Feel my Peace, be still

# Inspired

Listen to the utterances in your life bring them to words.

# Poetry Is A Notion

Poetry is a notion
From the soul of a man
It moves in one motion
Like the sea to the sand

Poetry is a notion
Like words from all about
They guide with great devotion
Full of faith without doubt

Poetry is a notion
To be seen to be heard
Things hidden become open
As thoughts are made to words

Poetry is a notion
Touching hearts lost and cold
It frees all emotions
Mends the spirit and soothes the soul

# Inspired

A conversation between you and your thoughts
come to life in words

# POETRY

Things seldom seen, things mostly heard
These are my thoughts, these are my words
I give them freely, to those who would hear
The sounds I bring about, the thoughts I make so clear

Deep I will take you, far from where you are
Past all the moons, above all the stars
When we reach the sacred place and gaze upon the view
You'll begin to see your grace, you'll understand it's all for you

For these words would have no meaning, if no one had to hear
There's something good in dreaming, stay far away from fear
If I lift you beyond your problems, take you out of grief or sin
It's because God gave me wisdom, to help him win again

Inspired

Be careful and wise about who you trust.

# TRUST

A perception you gained from your experience in life
A belief you held dear with all your might
Your Heart unbroken made love with every touch
As you learned to give and began to trust

So, you lived each day filled with utter delight
Imaginations ran wild without bounds day and night
No reason or suspicion abound thoughts of misdeeds or unjust
And so, you remained true and bound to your cause with unbiased trust

And yet you didn't understand the perception you held so true
There's no way into thoughts and desires of anyone but you
Believe in yourself and God; believe in others if you must
But remember to accept the outcome if you decide to trust

Pay close attention to your decisions, your choices must be wise
Let no one into your heart and then close your eyes
If you stumble find your strength to rise and lift yourself up
And remember to get in touch with your perception before you begin to trust

Inspired

The deepest thoughts of my life came from my experiences.
There are many that describe me.

# The Gospel According to Darryl

There is a journey of mind
body and soul treading life to become one in heaven and earth
Soul is the hue in man that feels and emotionalizes
perceptions and initiates reactions
Body is the vessel, the host incarnate, the miracle from within the womb
Mind transcends the body and soul
it is the hearer of utterances, the director of movement
Life is the endless or shall I say timeless cycle of trials of give and takes
Life will never stop giving or taking
this is a truth that one must quickly realize
Then he or she will begin to enjoy the journey in oneness and peace
So, if you have not reached this realization
listen closely to what I'm about to tell you
You must first begin to comprehend
separation from self as well as its reactions to life
You must become a seeker
watcher and walker in life's cycle and self's reactions
Understand that life cannot hurt you
but the self will try to lead you to believe it will
So that you begin to seek and provide self
with protection, as if you are a victim
As a seeker, watcher and walker you will begin to understand
how to flow in life's cycles
Jesus provided the perfect example of when
why and how to move with and within life
He's the master abnegator of self
he showed us the way and the will of our God sense
begin to seek and watch for Gods signs
and direction in your walk through life
Patiently allow life to correct itself and it will if you don't give into self
To trust and live in that which comes from his signs and
directions take patient practice
Patient reactions are the way of the wise
those who can hear God will wait

# SPEAK YOUR TRUTH ABOUT
# INSPIRATION

Which of the poems in this ACT inspired you the most?
How has this ACT encouraged you to speak the truth about inspiration in your life?

*You may ask me a question about this ACT or leave a thought at: darrylgaines.com/Books*

# Social Media and Bookings

Website: Darrylgaines.com
Contact Number: (832) 308-7808
Facebook: Darrylgainesempowers

*Speaking Engagements Contact*
Email: Darrylgainesempowers@gmail.com
Email: Bookdarrylgaines@gmail.com

Twitter: @darrylgaines25

Instagram: @darrylgainesempowers

DARRYL GAINES **FOUNDATION**
*Helping Others Pursue Excellence*

*The Darryl Gaines Foundation*
Website: Darrylgaines.com
Email: Darrylgainesfoundation@gmail.com

*Books by Darryl Gaines*
Website: Darrylgaines.com/Books

# ABOUT THE AUTHOR

Darryl C. Gaines, A former Kansas City Chief, NFL Football player, has been employed at NASA for 26 years at various Centers across the U.S. He is currently the Assistant to the Center Director at the Johnson Space Center in Houston, Texas. He has traveled across the world to Canada, Russia, Germany, Italy and Japan to help NASA build and maintain international relationships and to further space exploration.

From humble beginnings in Mobile, Alabama, he is a graduate of Mississippi Valley State University, and received his MBA from the Naval Post-Graduate School in Monterey California. He completed a fellowship at the University of Michigan studying Business Acumen for High Potential Leaders. He was inducted into the Mississippi Valley State University's Hall of Fame in 2017.

As a motivational speaker, he has talked to thousands of kids at Schools, Boys and Girls Clubs and Community Events about the importance of education, his career in the NFL as well as his career at NASA and the importance of pursuing careers in Science, Technology, Engineering, and Mathematics (STEM). He is a father, entrepreneur, philanthropist, volunteer, mentor, and educator.

He is a member of the Board of Directors for Communities in Schools Bay-Area in Houston Texas. He is also a member of the Board of Directors for the Gulf Coast Exploreum Science Center in Mobile Alabama.

For several years, he has written poetry and has now compiled them to create his first publication—*A Poetic Conversation*.

CPSIA information can be obtained
at www.ICGtesting.com
Printed in the USA
FSOW04n1907011117
40643FS